Accounting Ledger

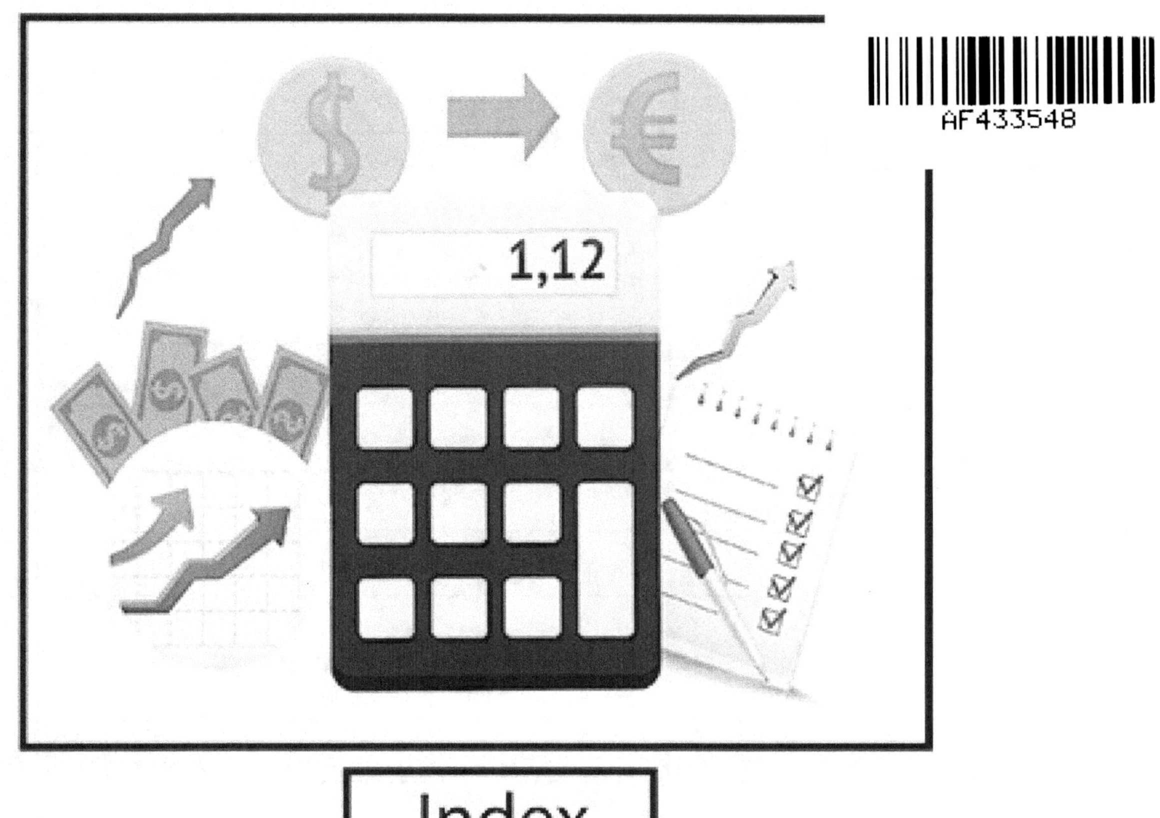

Index

⟹ *General Ledger*

⟹ *Chart of Accounts*

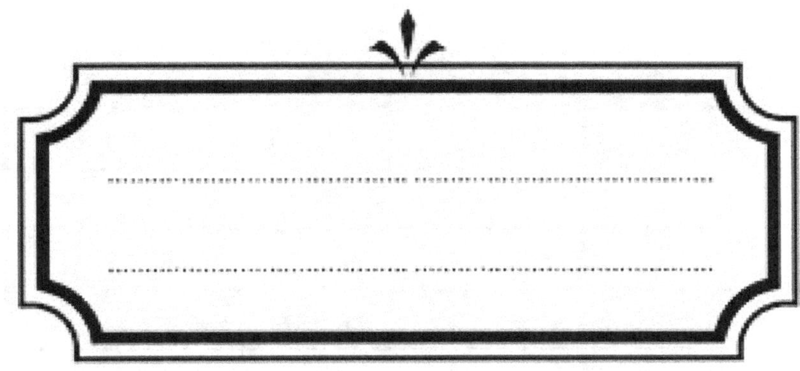

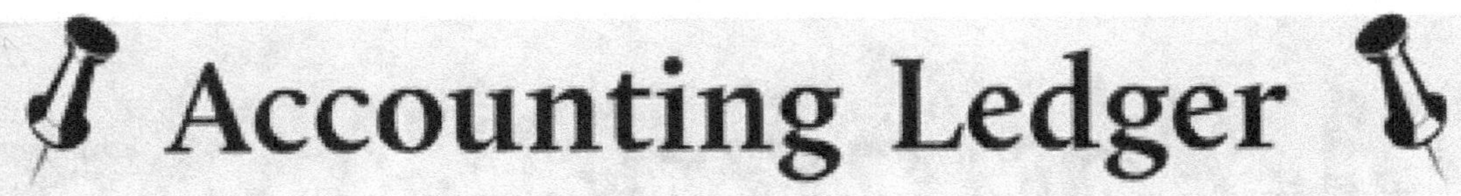

Accounting Ledger

Account Name : _______________________   sheet number : _______________________

Account Number : _______________________   Year : _______________________

DATE	ACCOUNT	DESCRIPTION	REF	DEBIT	CREDIT

Chart Of Account

Account	Account Name	Account Taype

Accounting Ledger

Account Name :   sheet number :

Account Number :   Year :

DATE	ACCOUNT	DESCRIPTION	REF	DEBIT	CREDIT

 Chart Of Account 

Account	Account Name	Account Taype

 Accounting Ledger

Account Name : _______________________   sheet number : _______________

Account Number : _______________________   Year : _______________

DATE	ACCOUNT	DESCRIPTION	REF	DEBIT	CREDIT

Chart Of Account  

Account	Account Name	Account Taype

 Accounting Ledger

Account Name : _______________________   sheet number : _______________________

Account Number : _______________________   Year : _______________________

DATE	ACCOUNT	DESCRIPTION	REF	DEBIT	CREDIT

 Chart Of Account 

Account	Account Name	Account Taype

Accounting Ledger

Account Name : ________________________   sheet number : ________________

Account Number : ________________________   Year : ________________

DATE	ACCOUNT	DESCRIPTION	REF	DEBIT	CREDIT

 Accounting Ledger

Account Name : ___________________________   **sheet number :** ___________

Account Number : ___________________________   **Year :** ___________

DATE	ACCOUNT	DESCRIPTION	REF	DEBIT	CREDIT

Accounting Ledger

Account Name : _______________________   sheet number : _______________

Account Number : _______________________   Year : _______________

DATE	ACCOUNT	DESCRIPTION	REF	DEBIT	CREDIT

Accounting Ledger

Account Name : _______________________   **sheet number :** _______________________

Account Number : _______________________   **Year :** _______________________

DATE	ACCOUNT	DESCRIPTION	REF	DEBIT	CREDIT

Accounting Ledger

Account Name : ______________________

sheet number : ______________________

Account Number : ______________________

Year : ______________________

DATE	ACCOUNT	DESCRIPTION	REF	DEBIT	CREDIT

Accounting Ledger

Account Name : ___________________________   sheet number : ___________

Account Number : ___________________   Year : ___________

DATE	ACCOUNT	DESCRIPTION	REF	DEBIT	CREDIT

Accounting Ledger

Account Name : ___________________________   sheet number : __________

Account Number : ___________________   Year : ___________________

DATE	ACCOUNT	DESCRIPTION	REF	DEBIT	CREDIT

Accounting Ledger

Account Name :

sheet number :

Account Number :

Year :

DATE	ACCOUNT	DESCRIPTION	REF	DEBIT	CREDIT

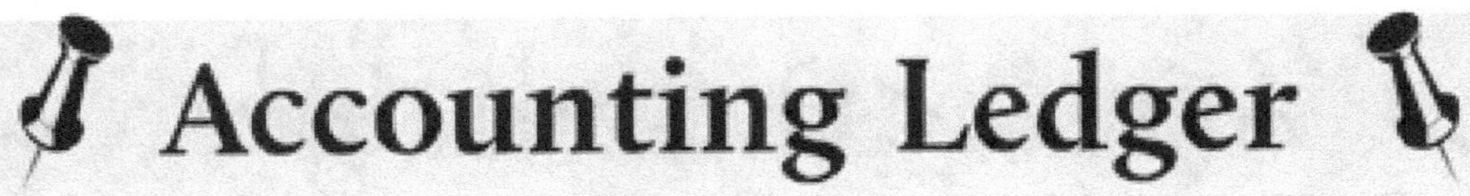

Accounting Ledger

Account Name :

sheet number :

Account Number :

Year :

DATE	ACCOUNT	DESCRIPTION	REF	DEBIT	CREDIT

Accounting Ledger

Account Name : ___________________________   sheet number : ___________

Account Number : ___________________________   Year : ___________

DATE	ACCOUNT	DESCRIPTION	REF	DEBIT	CREDIT

Accounting Ledger

Account Name : _______________________   sheet number : _______________

Account Number : _______________________   Year : _______________

DATE	ACCOUNT	DESCRIPTION	REF	DEBIT	CREDIT

Accounting Ledger

Account Name : _______________________

sheet number : _______________________

Account Number : _______________________

Year : _______________________

DATE	ACCOUNT	DESCRIPTION	REF	DEBIT	CREDIT

Accounting Ledger

Account Name : ______________________   sheet number : ______________

Account Number : _____________________   Year : ______________________

DATE	ACCOUNT	DESCRIPTION	REF	DEBIT	CREDIT

Accounting Ledger

Account Name : _______________________ **sheet number :** _______________

Account Number : _______________________ **Year :** _______________

DATE	ACCOUNT	DESCRIPTION	REF	DEBIT	CREDIT

Accounting Ledger

Account Name : ____________________   sheet number : ____________________

Account Number : ____________________   Year : ____________________

DATE	ACCOUNT	DESCRIPTION	REF	DEBIT	CREDIT

Accounting Ledger

Account Name : ________________________   sheet number : ________________

Account Number : ________________________   Year : ________________

DATE	ACCOUNT	DESCRIPTION	REF	DEBIT	CREDIT

Accounting Ledger

Account Name :   sheet number :

Account Number :   Year :

DATE	ACCOUNT	DESCRIPTION	REF	DEBIT	CREDIT

 Accounting Ledger

Account Name :

sheet number :

Account Number :

Year :

DATE	ACCOUNT	DESCRIPTION	REF	DEBIT	CREDIT

Accounting Ledger

Account Name : ___________________________   sheet number : ___________

Account Number : ___________________________   Year : ___________

DATE	ACCOUNT	DESCRIPTION	REF	DEBIT	CREDIT

 Accounting Ledger

Account Name :

sheet number :

Account Number :

Year :

DATE	ACCOUNT	DESCRIPTION	REF	DEBIT	CREDIT

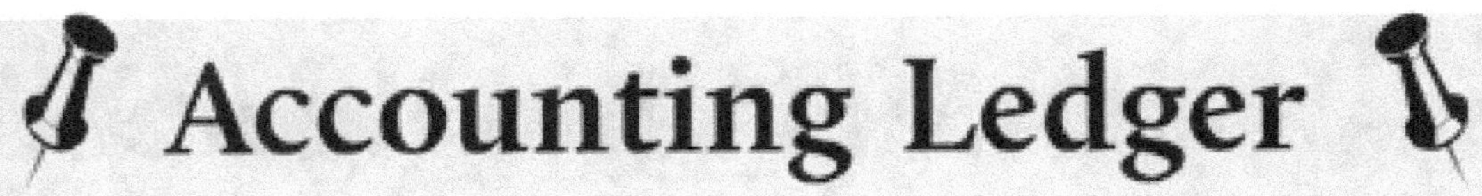

Accounting Ledger

Account Name :

sheet number :

Account Number :

Year :

DATE	ACCOUNT	DESCRIPTION	REF	DEBIT	CREDIT

Accounting Ledger

Account Name :   sheet number :

Account Number :   Year :

DATE	ACCOUNT	DESCRIPTION	REF	DEBIT	CREDIT

Accounting Ledger

Account Name : _______________________   sheet number : _______________

Account Number : _______________________   Year : _______________

DATE	ACCOUNT	DESCRIPTION	REF	DEBIT	CREDIT

Accounting Ledger

Account Name: ______________________ sheet number: ______________________

Account Number: ______________________ Year: ______________________

DATE	ACCOUNT	DESCRIPTION	REF	DEBIT	CREDIT

Accounting Ledger

Account Name :

sheet number :

Account Number :

Year :

DATE	ACCOUNT	DESCRIPTION	REF	DEBIT	CREDIT

Accounting Ledger

Account Name : __________________________   sheet number : __________

Account Number : __________________________   Year : __________

DATE	ACCOUNT	DESCRIPTION	REF	DEBIT	CREDIT

Accounting Ledger

Account Name :   sheet number :

Account Number :   Year :

DATE	ACCOUNT	DESCRIPTION	REF	DEBIT	CREDIT

Accounting Ledger

Account Name : _____________________   sheet number : _____________

Account Number : _____________________   Year : _____________

DATE	ACCOUNT	DESCRIPTION	REF	DEBIT	CREDIT

Accounting Ledger

Account Name : ___________________________   sheet number : ___________

Account Number : ___________________________   Year : ___________

DATE	ACCOUNT	DESCRIPTION	REF	DEBIT	CREDIT

Accounting Ledger

Account Name :

sheet number :

Account Number :

Year :

DATE	ACCOUNT	DESCRIPTION	REF	DEBIT	CREDIT

Accounting Ledger

Account Name : ______________________   sheet number : ______________________

Account Number : ______________________   Year : ______________________

DATE	ACCOUNT	DESCRIPTION	REF	DEBIT	CREDIT

Accounting Ledger

Account Name : ___________________________   sheet number : ___________________

Account Number : ___________________________   Year : ___________________

DATE	ACCOUNT	DESCRIPTION	REF	DEBIT	CREDIT

Accounting Ledger

Account Name : _______________________   sheet number : _______________

Account Number: _______________________   Year : _______________

DATE	ACCOUNT	DESCRIPTION	REF	DEBIT	CREDIT

Accounting Ledger

Account Name **:** ____________________   sheet number **:** ____________

Account Number **:** ____________________   Year **:** ____________

DATE	ACCOUNT	DESCRIPTION	REF	DEBIT	CREDIT

 Accounting Ledger

Account Name :   sheet number :

Account Number :   Year :

DATE	ACCOUNT	DESCRIPTION	REF	DEBIT	CREDIT

Accounting Ledger

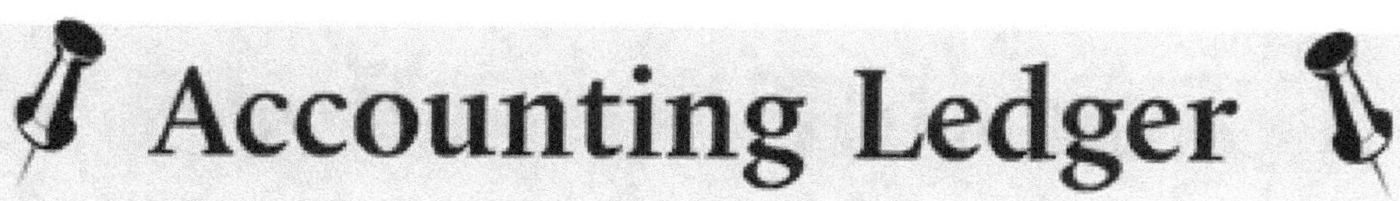

Account Name : _______________________   sheet number : _______________

Account Number : _______________________   Year : _______________

DATE	ACCOUNT	DESCRIPTION	REF	DEBIT	CREDIT

Accounting Ledger

Account Name : ________________________   sheet number : ________________________

Account Number : ________________________   Year : ________________________

DATE	ACCOUNT	DESCRIPTION	REF	DEBIT	CREDIT

Accounting Ledger

Account Name :

sheet number :

Account Number :

Year :

DATE	ACCOUNT	DESCRIPTION	REF	DEBIT	CREDIT

Accounting Ledger

Account Name :

sheet number :

Account Number :

Year :

DATE	ACCOUNT	DESCRIPTION	REF	DEBIT	CREDIT

Accounting Ledger

Account Name : ________________   sheet number : ________________

Account Number : ________________   Year : ________________

DATE	ACCOUNT	DESCRIPTION	REF	DEBIT	CREDIT

Account Name : _________________________   sheet number : _________________________

Account Number : _________________________   Year : _________________________

DATE	ACCOUNT	DESCRIPTION	REF	DEBIT	CREDIT

Accounting Ledger

Account Name : ___________________________   sheet number : ___________________

Account Number : ___________________________   Year : ___________________

DATE	ACCOUNT	DESCRIPTION	REF	DEBIT	CREDIT

Accounting Ledger

Account Name : _________________________   sheet number : _________

Account Number : _________________________   Year : _________

DATE	ACCOUNT	DESCRIPTION	REF	DEBIT	CREDIT

Accounting Ledger

Account Name : ___________________ sheet number : ___________________

Account Number : ___________________ Year : ___________________

DATE	ACCOUNT	DESCRIPTION	REF	DEBIT	CREDIT

Accounting Ledger

Account Name : _______________________   sheet number : _______________

Account Number : _______________________   Year : _______________

DATE	ACCOUNT	DESCRIPTION	REF	DEBIT	CREDIT

Accounting Ledger

Account Name : ___________________________   sheet number : ___________

Account Number : ___________________________   Year : ___________

DATE	ACCOUNT	DESCRIPTION	REF	DEBIT	CREDIT

Accounting Ledger

Account Name : _______________________   sheet number : _______________

Account Number : _______________________   Year : _______________

DATE	ACCOUNT	DESCRIPTION	REF	DEBIT	CREDIT

 Accounting Ledger

Account Name : ______________________   **sheet number :** ______________________

Account Number : ______________________   **Year :** ______________________

DATE	ACCOUNT	DESCRIPTION	REF	DEBIT	CREDIT

Accounting Ledger

Account Name : ___________________________   sheet number : __________

Account Number : ___________________________   Year : __________

DATE	ACCOUNT	DESCRIPTION	REF	DEBIT	CREDIT

Accounting Ledger

Account Name :

sheet number :

Account Number :

Year :

DATE	ACCOUNT	DESCRIPTION	REF	DEBIT	CREDIT

Accounting Ledger

Account Name :

sheet number :

Account Number :

Year :

DATE	ACCOUNT	DESCRIPTION	REF	DEBIT	CREDIT

Accounting Ledger

Account Name : _______________________   sheet number : _______________________

Account Number : _______________________   Year : _______________________

DATE	ACCOUNT	DESCRIPTION	REF	DEBIT	CREDIT

Accounting Ledger

Account Name :

sheet number :

Account Number :

Year :

DATE	ACCOUNT	DESCRIPTION	REF	DEBIT	CREDIT

Accounting Ledger

Account Name :

sheet number :

Account Number :

Year :

DATE	ACCOUNT	DESCRIPTION	REF	DEBIT	CREDIT

Accounting Ledger

Account Name : _______________________

sheet number : _______________________

Account Number : _______________________

Year : _______________________

DATE	ACCOUNT	DESCRIPTION	REF	DEBIT	CREDIT

Accounting Ledger

Account Name : ___________________________ **sheet number :** ___________

Account Number : _________________________ **Year :** ___________________

DATE	ACCOUNT	DESCRIPTION	REF	DEBIT	CREDIT

Accounting Ledger

Account Name : ___________________   sheet number : ___________

Account Number : _________________   Year : ___________________

DATE	ACCOUNT	DESCRIPTION	REF	DEBIT	CREDIT

 Accounting Ledger

Account Name : _______________________   sheet number : _______________________

Account Number : _______________________   Year : _______________________

DATE	ACCOUNT	DESCRIPTION	REF	DEBIT	CREDIT

Accounting Ledger

Account Name : _______________________   sheet number : _______________

Account Number : _______________________   Year : _______________

DATE	ACCOUNT	DESCRIPTION	REF	DEBIT	CREDIT

Accounting Ledger

Account Name :

sheet number :

Account Number :

Year :

DATE	ACCOUNT	DESCRIPTION	REF	DEBIT	CREDIT

Accounting Ledger

Account Name : ___________________________   sheet number : ___________

Account Number : ___________________________   Year : ___________

DATE	ACCOUNT	DESCRIPTION	REF	DEBIT	CREDIT

Accounting Ledger

Account Name :

sheet number :

Account Number :

Year :

DATE	ACCOUNT	DESCRIPTION	REF	DEBIT	CREDIT

Accounting Ledger

Account Name : _______________________

sheet number : _______________

Account Number : _______________________

Year : _______________

DATE	ACCOUNT	DESCRIPTION	REF	DEBIT	CREDIT

Accounting Ledger

Account Name : ___________________________   sheet number : ___________

Account Number : ___________________________   Year : ___________

DATE	ACCOUNT	DESCRIPTION	REF	DEBIT	CREDIT

 Accounting Ledger

Account Name : ____________________   sheet number : ____________________

Account Number : ____________________   Year : ____________________

DATE	ACCOUNT	DESCRIPTION	REF	DEBIT	CREDIT

Accounting Ledger

Account Name : _______________________   **sheet number :** _______________________

Account Number : _______________________   **Year :** _______________________

DATE	ACCOUNT	DESCRIPTION	REF	DEBIT	CREDIT

Accounting Ledger

Account Name : ___________________________   sheet number : ___________________

Account Number : _________________________   Year : ___________________________

DATE	ACCOUNT	DESCRIPTION	REF	DEBIT	CREDIT

Accounting Ledger

Account Name : _______________________   sheet number : _______________________

Account Number : _______________________   Year : _______________________

DATE	ACCOUNT	DESCRIPTION	REF	DEBIT	CREDIT

Accounting Ledger

Account Name : ________________________   sheet number : ________________________

Account Number : ________________________   Year : ________________________

DATE	ACCOUNT	DESCRIPTION	REF	DEBIT	CREDIT

Accounting Ledger

Account Name : __________________________   sheet number : __________________

Account Number : __________________   Year : __________________

DATE	ACCOUNT	DESCRIPTION	REF	DEBIT	CREDIT

Accounting Ledger

Account Name : _______________________   **sheet number :** _______________

Account Number : _______________________   **Year :** _______________

DATE	ACCOUNT	DESCRIPTION	REF	DEBIT	CREDIT

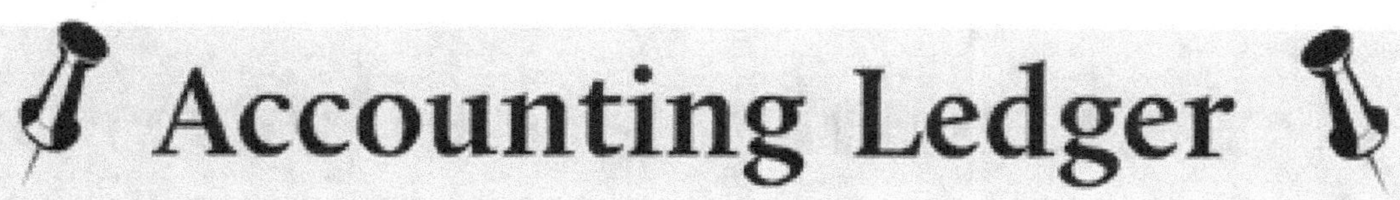

Accounting Ledger

Account Name : _______________________   sheet number : _______________________

Account Number : _______________________   Year : _______________________

DATE	ACCOUNT	DESCRIPTION	REF	DEBIT	CREDIT

Accounting Ledger

Account Name :

sheet number :

Account Number :

Year :

DATE	ACCOUNT	DESCRIPTION	REF	DEBIT	CREDIT

Accounting Ledger

Account Name : ___________________   sheet number : ___________

Account Number : ___________________   Year : ___________

DATE	ACCOUNT	DESCRIPTION	REF	DEBIT	CREDIT

Accounting Ledger

Account Name : __________________________   sheet number : __________

Account Number : __________________________   Year : __________

DATE	ACCOUNT	DESCRIPTION	REF	DEBIT	CREDIT

Accounting Ledger

Account Name : ___________________________   sheet number : ___________

Account Number : _________________________   Year : ___________________

DATE	ACCOUNT	DESCRIPTION	REF	DEBIT	CREDIT

Accounting Ledger

Account Name : _______________________   sheet number : _______________________

Account Number : _______________________   Year : _______________________

DATE	ACCOUNT	DESCRIPTION	REF	DEBIT	CREDIT

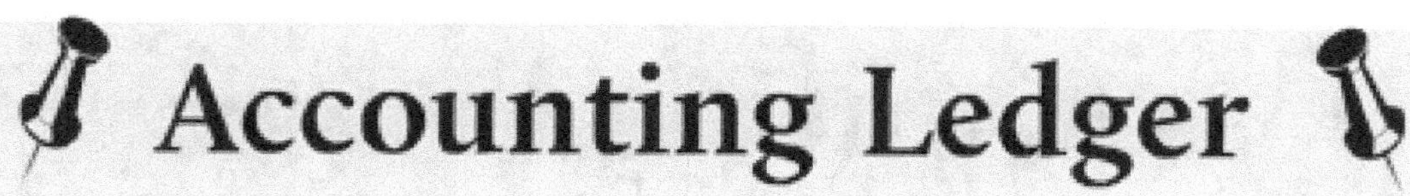

Accounting Ledger

Account Name : _______________________   sheet number : _______________________

Account Number : _______________________   Year : _______________________

DATE	ACCOUNT	DESCRIPTION	REF	DEBIT	CREDIT

Accounting Ledger

Account Name : _______________________   sheet number : _______________________

Account Number : _______________________   Year : _______________________

DATE	ACCOUNT	DESCRIPTION	REF	DEBIT	CREDIT

Accounting Ledger

Account Name : _______________________   sheet number : _______________

Account Number : _______________________   Year : _______________

DATE	ACCOUNT	DESCRIPTION	REF	DEBIT	CREDIT

Accounting Ledger

Account Name : _______________________   **sheet number :** _______________________

Account Number : _______________________   **Year :** _______________________

DATE	ACCOUNT	DESCRIPTION	REF	DEBIT	CREDIT

Accounting Ledger

Account Name :   sheet number :

Account Number :   Year :

DATE	ACCOUNT	DESCRIPTION	REF	DEBIT	CREDIT

Accounting Ledger

Account Name : _______________________ **sheet number :** _______________

Account Number : _______________________ **Year :** _______________

DATE	ACCOUNT	DESCRIPTION	REF	DEBIT	CREDIT

 Chart Of Account 

Account	Account Name	Account Taype

Chart Of Account

Account	Account Name	Account Taype

Chart Of Account

Account	Account Name	Account Taype

Chart Of Account

Account	Account Name	Account Taype

Chart Of Account

Account	Account Name	Account Taype

Chart Of Account

Account	Account Name	Account Taype

Chart Of Account  

Account	Account Name	Account Taype

Chart Of Account  

Account	Account Name	Account Taype

Chart Of Account

Account	Account Name	Account Taype

Chart Of Account

Account	Account Name	Account Taype

Chart Of Account

Account	Account Name	Account Taype